Rickey & Joan McDermott

Untapped Miracles for Tapped-Out Christians

Spectacular Energy Sources for the Body of Christ

ADULT JOURNAL

*Dedicated to the many churches that faithfully
stood by us even during the hard times—an outstanding
example being the Fremont Community Church*

CONTENTS

This journal was created with input from more than 40 pastors and laypersons from across North America.

Writing team: David R. Mains (Director of The Chapel Ministries), Patric Knaak, Laurie Mains, Marian Oliver, Randy Petersen, Mitchell Vander Vorst

Cover Illustration: Joe VanSeveren
Cover and Text Design: Blum Graphic Design

Copyright © 1997 by Mainstay Church Resources
Published by Mainstay Church Resources

Scripture quotations marked (NLT) are taken from the *Holy Bible,* New Living Translation, copyright © 1996. Used by permission of Tyndale House Publishers, Inc., Wheaton, Illinois 60189. All rights reserved.

Scripture quotations marked (NIV) are taken from the HOLY BIBLE, NEW INTERNATIONAL VERSION®. NIV®. Copyright © 1973, 1978, 1984 by International Bible Society. Used by permission of Zondervan Publishing House. All rights reserved.

Mainstay Church Resources is a new publishing outreach of The Chapel of the Air Ministries. Our goal is to facilitate revival among God's people by helping them develop healthy spiritual habits in nine vital areas that always characterize genuine times of spiritual awakening. To support this goal, Mainstay Church Resources provides practical tools and resources including the annual 50-Day Spiritual Adventure, the Seasonal Advent Celebration, and the 4-Week Festival of Worship.

Printed in the United States of America
ISBN 1-57849-038-3

INTRODUCTION

"Hi. How are you?"

"Busy."

You've been hearing that more and more lately, haven't you? People are busy with their jobs, their family obligations, their hobbies, their computers. Even the things they do for fun keep them hopping. And if they have kids, they're chauffeuring them somewhere all the time.

For Christians, add a full slate of church activities—worship services, committee meetings, Bible studies.

It's ironic, but the very things that supposedly keep us fresh often wear us out.

But there may be another reason we Christians feel weary. We see a culture around us that appears less friendly to Christianity every day. It seems harder and harder for us to stay holy, to let our light shine in a dim world. We feel embattled by the issues of our time. We're working hard to be a positive influence, but it doesn't seem to do much good.

And so we're tired, run down, tapped out.

Hey, that's an upbeat way to start a new 50-Day Adventure: "How exhausted are you?" But if you're honest, you'll probably admit it's true. What you need more than anything right now is *energy, spiritual energy!*

TRUE STORY: One of our writers, in the heat of last summer, made the mistake of plugging a hair dryer into the same circuit as his air conditioner, tripping the circuit breaker. He lived in an apartment in an old house, so with the help of his elderly landlord, he found a fuse box in the cellar and flipped the switches. Nothing happened. The power was still off.

It was a Saturday morning, and all the electricians in town had gone to the beach, so our poor writer suffered and sweltered in his dark apartment all weekend.

Monday morning an electrician showed up, checked the old fuse box, and asked the landlord, "Are there any other fuse boxes in the house?"

"Oh, yeah," the old man replied. "Up in the apartment. In the kitchen closet."

Our writer had been unaware of this location. Sure enough, the electrician flipped one switch and the power came on.

There's a lesson in this. Our writer (let's call him George, though his real name is Randy) spent a miserable weekend in the dark—*even though he was sitting a few feet away from the switch that would easily restore his power!* The power was there all the time; he just wasn't tapping into it.

Spiritually speaking, we often do the same thing. We have ready power within our reach, but we feel powerless. How do we tap into the energy we need?

You probably know some people who always appear to be spiritually energized. (Maybe you're one of those individuals.) During the next 50 days we'll share some of their secrets. We'll explore eight untapped miracles, habits that can give our spiritual lives renewed vitality, no matter where we are on the energy scale.

We're not trying to create Super-Christians. And we're not offering instant answers, just time-tested, biblically rooted practices that have immense value for individuals and churches today. We believe God's miracles are all around us, waiting to be enjoyed. So let's tap in! Here are the miracles we'll focus on during this Adventure. You'll read more about them as you go through this journal.

◆ Untapped Miracle #1: Finding Tension's Good Side
◆ Untapped Miracle #2: The 24/7 Church
◆ Untapped Miracle #3: Christian Hospitality
◆ Untapped Miracle #4: Pulpit/Pew Mutual Support
◆ Untapped Miracle #5: Prayer with Fasting
◆ Untapped Miracle #6: Telling Our Stories
◆ Untapped Miracle #7: The Wider Kingship
◆ Untapped Miracle #8: The Living Christ

How Should I Use This Journal?

This is more than an ordinary booklet you're holding. It's a guide for accelerated spiritual growth. It's a road map to lead you on a Spiritual Adventure that can change your life. We trust that two months from now, as you've allowed God's Spirit to work, you will be different—a stronger, healthier, more energized Christian.

More than half a million people will be going on this Spiritual Adventure with you. Thousands of churches will benefit as the Lord touches individual lives like yours. And all of that starts as you turn these pages and begin to study the Scriptures, pray, and put into practice the action steps in this journal. There's a lot going on here, but don't be overwhelmed. Just take the Adventure one step at a time, and you'll be fine.

What do I need to go on the 50-Day Spiritual Adventure?

1. Your Bible. Each day we suggest a passage of Scripture for you to read. Regular Scripture reading is an important part of this Adventure, an untapped miracle energy source of its own. Make sure you're using a Bible you can understand.

2. This journal. Here is where you'll be processing what you're reading in Scripture each day. We offer a few questions to help you get at the meaning of the text and how it applies to your life. This journal is not an intensive Bible study guide; it's primarily a tool for life application. Along with the daily Scripture questions, you'll find instructions for action steps that will help you live out the biblical principles you're learning.

3. The Adventure Guidebook—*When the Troops Are Tired,* by Dr. David Mains. This essential book will help you better understand the eight themes of the Adventure, giving you the big picture of untapped miracles you (and perhaps your church) are tapping into. Read a chapter a week to keep current (reading time: maybe half an hour per chapter). To obtain the book or audiobook, contact your church, your local Christian bookstore, or Mainstay Church Resources, the publishing outreach of The Chapel Ministries. See page 18 for more information.

4. A good attitude. This Adventure will stretch you if you're open to spiritual growth. Take it seriously, but not too seriously! Have fun with the Adventure, and let God work within you to develop some healthy new spiritual habits.

WHAT DO I NEED TO DO?

There are assignments for you to complete each day of the Adventure. First, you'll need to read the suggested Scripture passage in your Bible and answer the questions in the journal. We recommend also that you choose some Bible verses to memorize. One per week is a good goal to shoot for. *The Tapped-Out Christian's Energy Pack* contains 23 verses for you to choose from, selections that should give your spiritual life a power boost.

Second, you will need to read a chapter every week in the Adventure Guidebook, *When the Troops Are Tired* by Dr. David Mains. And then there are the action steps. . . .

WHAT ARE THESE ACTION STEPS?

They're specific activities we're suggesting you do to apply the Adventure themes to your life. The next few pages will explain the steps thoroughly. The first action step is a daily prayer. That's easy enough, but it sets the tone for everything else in the Adventure.

The second action step involves being attentive to God's "24/7" presence in your life—24 hours a day, 7 days a week. For the third step, you'll plan a time to extend simple Christian hospitality. The fourth step is a matter of connecting with your pastor or church leader through prayer and helpful feedback. With the fifth step, you'll take your spiritual life to a new level by reclaiming the time-proven discipline of prayer with fasting.

The Adventure works well when you follow our suggestions, but you may choose to customize the steps to fit your situation. If one of the steps is driving you crazy, forget it and focus on the others. Better to have four important life changes than five noble attempts cut short by a nervous breakdown! Or, if you can handle more, do it! (For a quick overview of all the Adventure assignments, see p. 18.)

How much time commitment is involved here?

We estimate it will take just 10–15 minutes per day to complete the daily journal assignments. Reading the guidebook should take an extra half hour per week. And you'll need a few additional time blocks during the 50-day period to complete some action steps.

Does that sound like too much? We hope not. As with any important relationship, it's hard to grow closer to Christ if we don't devote at least a minimal amount of time to him each day.

How do I keep track of all the stuff I need to do?

We will prompt you throughout this journal with check boxes to help you keep current with the action steps. For a quick overview of where you've been and where you're headed each week, see the "Looking Back ... Moving Forward" pages, usually after each Friday journal page. It might be helpful also to put some notes on your personal calendar about the bigger things you'll be doing.

Do I need to follow the journal every day?

Yes. But if you miss a day or two, don't panic! It's best to pick up the journal entries with the current day, rather than try to make up days you've skipped.

What's different about Saturday/Sunday pages?

Each of the eight themes is introduced with a format different from the other journal pages. On weekends, a commentary by Dr. David Mains sets the tone for the days that follow.

Can I do the Adventure with my friends or family?

Absolutely. That's a great way to make it even more meaningful. This will take some extra time as you discuss the scriptures or review one another's progress on the action steps, but the mutual encouragement and accountability will be of great benefit. And we provide lots of help with journals for adults, students, and children, along with small group materials. For specific ideas, get the pamphlet *Adventuring with Friends and Family* from your church, or call Mainstay Church Resources at 1-800-224-2735.

What if I want a more in-depth study?

We've suggested some ways for you to go deeper and customize the Adventure to meet your needs. On each "Looking Back ... Moving Forward" page, you'll find optional follow-up scriptures and a recommended book for further reading on the topic of the week. We've reviewed dozens of titles and believe these are the best available on the Adventure themes.

WHAT CAN I DO TO KEEP GOING WHEN THE ADVENTURE IS OVER?

Once you've finished the Adventure, you may want to continue with some of the spiritual habits you've developed over these 50 days. On page 76 we offer some great ideas to help you keep going.

CAN I FOLLOW THE ADVENTURE ON RADIO?

You bet. Many participants will benefit from the two-minute "Adventure Highlight" carried on numerous radio stations throughout North America. To find out where and when to tune in, call Mainstay Church Resources at 1-800-224-2735.

WHERE SHOULD I START?

Familiarize yourself with the five action steps on pages 8–17. You might also flip through the day-to-day section of the journal starting on page 22. Then, to give yourself a head start, begin the Warm-Up Day exercises on page 19.

It's About Real Life

The *Life Application Study Bible* features over 10,000 Life Application notes to help you apply the truth of God's Word to everyday life. In addition, this best-selling study Bible contains everything you need to thoroughly study God's Word, including book introductions, personality profiles, in-text maps, a dictionary/concordance, and more. Available in the accurate and easy-to-understand New Living Translation.

To obtain a *Life Application Study Bible*, New Living Translation, use the order form on page 78. Or, call weekdays toll-free: 1-800-224-2735 (U.S.), 1-800-461-4114 (Canada).

ACTION STEP
1

ADDRESS YOUR TENSION TO GOD'S ATTENTION

Wouldn't it be great if you could have a life totally free from stress? No tensions, no concerns, nothing to make your heart race?

Well, actually, there is a condition like that. It's called death.

The fact is, on *this* side of the hereafter, life is full of tension. Jesus himself promised, "Here on earth you will have many trials and sorrows" (John 16:33b, NLT). It's a given.

We face some tensions simply because that's the way our culture is. You may get cut off in traffic by a reckless driver. You may get audited by the IRS. You may lose your job.

As a Christian, you may feel additional tension because people don't understand or accept your faith. Co-workers may mock you or go out of their way to offend. You may feel tension as you see society slipping into immorality.

Other tensions exist because we are fallen human beings prone to sin. We struggle with Paul in his Romans 7 situation—we want to do good but keep choosing evil.

Sometimes it's exactly those tensions that Christ uses to get us where he wants us to be. We tend to focus on the problem—how bad we're feeling, how our frustrating circumstances have kept us from living as we'd envisioned. But God sees "the other bank of the river." He knows we will learn patience and humility while sitting through that hour-long traffic jam and sheepishly showing up late for work. He understands that a period of unemployment just might push us to try a different career in which he can best use us, or that a broken engagement will help us examine how much we depend on the love of another person, rather than on his divine love for us.

We're not saying the Lord expects us to avoid mourning our losses, or that he orchestrates horrible circumstances in our lives so we have to take the long, hard way toward his plan for us. Bad things do happen—to good people and bad people alike—because there is sin in the world. But Christ is our Redeemer, and that doesn't just mean he will save us at the end of time. It means he's working to save us in every situation, right here, right now. The tensions we're up against can actually be "bought back" and used to the kingdom's advantage.

The implication is clear. Those mind-boggling, soul-stretching, body-exhausting circumstances have a flip side *when we let Christ redeem them the way he wants to.* So that's the focus of our first action step. Get in the habit of gathering your tensions and—not fretting, not plotting revenge—but releasing them to God. Then look for the ways the Lord will use those experiences to change his world, his church, or you his child for the better.

WHAT2DO: We all have a tendency to complain and worry about our tensions. So it will take a lot of prayer to begin noticing the good God is working in our behalf. Once a day, pray the Tension's Good Side Prayer. After several days you may start to put it in your own words, but try to follow this basic pattern, filling in the tension that immediately jumps to mind when you come to the blank space. Don't just launch this prayer to the Lord; take time to listen for his response. How could he be directing you in the midst of your tense situations? What might he say to help you relax in his presence? You can learn a lot (and change a lot!) in these quiet moments with him.

The Tension's Good Side Prayer

Lord,
One of the untapped miracles in this
Adventure is to see how you bring
good out of our tensions.
Right now, a tension I'm facing personally
is _____.
I turn this situation over to you, knowing
you love me and are in control of my days.
Help me to live believing you are constantly
working in my behalf.
And let me be on the lookout today for
evidences of your miracle touch.
Amen

ACTION STEP

2

A generation ago, the 7-11 chain made its name by being open for business from 7 A.M. all the way to 11 P.M. In those days, that seemed like a long time.

Now, of course, not only convenience stores but most supermarkets do business at least that long, and some are open nonstop. They've learned that customers want to be able to count on a store to be there when they need it—24 hours a day, 7 days a week.

Some Christians have been doing business the old way. They focus on their faith for a few hours on Sunday morning, maybe a few more on Sunday evening, and they might even have another church event during the week. But when they leave the church building, they close up shop and go back to everyday life until the next church service. We're not saying they stop behaving like Christians (though some do). The problem is, they stop thinking about it. They spend the rest of the week preoccupied with the demands of everyday living.

But God's power isn't cooped up in a building, and it's certainly not restricted to one day a week. Miracles can happen to us and through us every day—at work, at play, on the subway, on the highway.

We need to put out a "We never close" sign so people can count on us to be God's representatives 24 hours a day, 7 days a week. We'll be energized as we remember that "God never closes," that we can depend on his 24/7 presence.

WHAT2DO: Each day of the Adventure, play the "To, Through, and Talk About" game. This should be a fun way to remind yourself that the body of Christ is active 24/7—that God ministers to and through us all week. The game has three simple rules:

1. Ask yourself, "How did God minister *to* me today?" This could be, for example, an answer to prayer, an insight from the Word, or a helpful conversation with a friend.

2. Then ask yourself, "How did God minister *through* me today?" Did he use you to encourage someone? Did he help you choose to do what was right in an uncomfortable situation? How were you the body of Christ today?

3. Consider how you could *talk about* some of your 24/7 "miracles." This will allow you and those you talk with to celebrate what God is doing in your midst. Aim to do this *talk about* step at least five times during the Adventure.

Each day record either a *to* or *through* experience on the chart on pages 40–41. It may take a while for you to recognize these 24/7 "miracles," but keep at it. As with any game (or spiritual discipline), you'll improve with practice. Then, five times during the Adventure, circle one of the entries on your chart and *talk about* it with someone.

Be sure to remember the three *T*'s: *To*, *Through*, and *T*alk About. They'll become hallmarks of the 24/7 church.

REVEREND SPILLMAN'S IDEA OF COMMUNITY INVOLVEMENT WAS VASTLY DIFFERENT FROM THAT OF THE CHURCH BOARD.

ACTION STEP 3

When Jim and Sandy bought their house, they knew it needed work. An eccentric old man had lived there for years, letting the place fall to pieces. But Jim and Sandy were ready to roll up their sleeves—and so were some of their fellow church members who lived nearby. It became a team effort as church work crews scrubbed and painted and scraped and pounded. Others helped with the move, carting furniture, boxes, and bags into the fixed-up house. The neighbors looked on, glad that the neighborhood eyesore was getting a facelift.

Through the whole restoration process, Sandy and Jim were praying, "Lord, show us why you have brought us here. How can we use this home for you?"

Once they had settled into the house, they began to open it up to their neighbors, asking them over for dinners, birthday parties, and barbecues. They launched a Bible study and invited their new friends from the community as well as church friends.

They especially befriended one couple. The wife, Marilyn, said she was an atheist, but she still liked to chat about spiritual issues. She appreciated the fact that Sandy and Jim weren't pushy, that they gently expressed themselves but didn't force their beliefs on her.

After many casual get-togethers and some interesting discussions, Sandy felt God wanted her to press the issue: "Marilyn, would you like to commit yourself to Christ?"

"Yes," Marilyn replied. "You know, when I saw all those people from your church working on the house and moving you in, I knew you all had something I didn't have. And when you listened and tried to answer my questions without imposing what you believed on me, I was sure of it."[*]

God had used a home to welcome a new child into his family. It wasn't any preaching Jim and Sandy did or any philosophical brilliance; they merely opened their hearts and their home to Marilyn.

As we seek to have a powerful impact on our world, we often slam the door on one of the greatest resources we have. Christians in New Testament times knew their homes were as important as any other meeting place. In today's inhospitable world, Christian homes are miracles to be shared. So let's open them to what God wants to do through us to make others feel welcome and wanted.

[*]Story adapted from *Open Heart, Open Home* by Karen Mains (1997), pages 145–146. Used by permission of Mainstay Church Resources.

WHAT2DO: Consider how God can use your home. Could it be a place where people in your church gather to build a solid, caring community? Like Sandy and Jim, can you help some seeker find Christ in your home's nonthreatening environment? Or might the Lord be urging you to shelter someone in need within its warm, sturdy rooms?

At least once during this Adventure, invite others into your home for coffee, dessert, or a simple meal. Talk with God about whom to welcome—whether it's a single person, a couple, a family, or a group of folks from different walks of life.

Now, don't especially emphasize the food you serve or the way your house looks. It's hard to be hospitable if you're worried about how you appear to others. Remember what happened at the home in Bethany when busybody Martha complained that her sister Mary was simply sitting at Jesus' feet? "Martha, Martha," the Lord said gently, "Only one thing is needed. Mary has chosen what is better" (Luke 10:41–42, NIV).

Instead, focus on what happens as you talk with and listen to your guests. Let your "work" be making the conversation truly meaningful—a way to minister to one another. Here are some questions you might ask:

If you could get free plane tickets to any place in the world, where would you like to go, and why?

What would you like to be doing ten years from now?

Tell me about one day from your past that you'd like to live over again.

If you could have any problem in your life resolved, what would you want to change? (Save this question for people you know pretty well.)

How do you feel you're doing spiritually these days? (This question may not be appropriate for everyone.)

You'll find additional practical help and an in-depth study on this subject in Karen Mains's best-selling hospitality classic *Open Heart, Open Home.* You may be able to borrow a copy from your church, or you can order your own by calling 1-800-224-2735 (in Canada: 1-800-461-4114).

If it's not possible for you to open your own home, you might co-host a get-together with someone else. Maybe you could provide some of the food, or even help delegate responsibilities for a potluck meal. If you absolutely *can't* find a home to meet in, don't pass this action step by. Gather a group together and employ the same principles of hospitality at a nearby restaurant or picnic facility.

Whatever you decide to do, see how making connections with others can revitalize your sense of community and spark the fire of your spirit. And let that provoke you to further extend Christ's welcome by inviting others through your open door.

ACTION STEP
4
CONNECT WITH YOUR PASTOR

Just recently there was news about a big-city mayor who made a point of going around town asking folks, "How am I doing?" He knew he needed feedback in order to stay on track, and people freely offered it to him.

Auto manufacturers now have consumers test their new ideas for cars before those cars ever see a dealership. What these companies have learned is that the best way to make a good car is to ask people what they need.

Communication like that is a two-way street. One side asks for feedback and the other side honestly gives it. But what does this have to do with our churches?

Once upon a time, a church board decided to ask its pastor to resign. One elder broke the news to the pastor, who was shocked.

"But why?" the pastor protested. "I thought I was doing fine."

"Do you want the truth?"

"Of course."

"We all love you, Rev," the elder began. "That's what makes this so hard. But it's your preaching. People have been complaining. They say it's boring, too academic—they don't get anything out of it, and they can't connect it with their lives."

The pastor was dumbfounded. "That's not what they tell me! Every week as they file out, they tell me what a great sermon it was."

There's a serious crisis here. We might call it The Preaching Gap. But before you start putting all the blame on your pastor, remember, it's a two-way street.

- ◆ People usually don't spend enough time in prayer for their pastor.
- ◆ People seldom tell their pastor much about their lives—that is, about the cutting-edge issues they face in their daily work and in their homes. (This makes it hard for the pastor to know what everyone's needs are.)
- ◆ People make general complimentary comments to the pastor, even when they complain to others.
- ◆ People often forget about the sermon once they leave church—they never discuss it or try to apply it to their lives.
- ◆ People seldom give specific feedback on which parts of a sermon got through to them and which didn't.
- ◆ Pastors don't always know how to seek this feedback.

When the Word of God goes forth in a church service, it should be a team effort. The preacher delivers the message, but the people have to listen, take the sermon home with them, and incorporate it in their lives. When we help each other do this effectively, we will find that the sermons we hear will provide energy for the rest of the week.

WHAT2DO: Wouldn't it be great to come away from church saying, "Yes!"? To know your pastor was preaching directly to your needs? Do you long to hear sermons you can easily apply to your everyday life? Help make that happen by connecting with your pastor.

Start with prayer. For the first three weeks of the Adventure, make it a point to pray for your pastor, especially before and during the sermon. Pray also for yourself, that you will hear God's message to you in the pastor's words.

Then, during those first three weeks, make a special effort to put your pastor's words (and God's words) into action. Think about how each message is changing your life.

You don't have to stop all of this in the fourth week—these are great habits to hang on to—but now it's time for something else. Before the end of the Adventure, write a letter (or e-mail) to your pastor. This is an opportunity for you to offer your pastor some insights into your life and what you need to hear. Here are some thoughts you might share:

A way you've influenced my life is _____.

Something you said that I've put into action is _____.

A question I have is _____.

If you could speak about _____, that would be helpful to me.

NOTE: This is not the time to offer negative criticism of your pastor or the preaching. Be positive and practical in your feedback. Your goal is to help your pastor better understand your needs and those of your church family.

15

ACTION STEP 5

PROTESTER STARTS HUNGER STRIKE
Vows Not to Eat Until Conditions Change

A headline like that may impress you or appall you, depending on whether you think the "conditions" need changing. People have announced hunger strikes for all sorts of political and social causes. Going without food is often a desperate attempt to gain attention, putting pressure on leaders to change their policies.

So, whether you agree with the cause or not, you have to admit that a hunger striker is serious about it—dead serious. To say publicly, "What I believe in is more important than even food" . . . well, that certainly makes an impression.

Among Christians, fasting should never be anything like a hunger strike, but it still seems to be a way to show we mean business. Face it: prayer can be rather easy to do. But prayer *and fasting*? Do I care that much about what I'm praying for? Enough to miss a meal or two?

Some Christians shy away from fasting because it seems like a "work" we try to do to earn God's favor. And Jesus chided the Pharisees for making their fasts a public spectacle, showing themselves to be spiritual giants (Matthew 6:16–18). But Jesus himself fasted in the desert before his temptation (Matthew 4:2), and countless believers—in Scripture and in centuries since—have practiced it. Fasting seems to bring a certain spiritual power and energy to our prayer lives.

How does that work? We don't really know. It's not a magical ritual that forces God's hand. But it does seem to bring us to a point of greater commitment. When we honor God by putting time with him ahead of even eating, he honors us.

Just as a hunger striker focuses attention on a particular cause, so we can focus our attention on God's power and focus God's power on a situation that needs changing. And this change often happens in us, and then through us.

WHAT2DO: Do you have intense spiritual longings? Is there a situation for you, your church, or your community, in which you need God's direction?

At least once during the Adventure, practice a fast as part of your prayer life. Since fasting is a very personal thing and there are some cautions, we offer the following options:

1. **The lunch-to-lunch juice fast.** This is the best entry-level option, and we highly recommend it for those who have not fasted before. Eat a healthy meal,

including fruits and vegetables, for lunch one day. Then skip supper and breakfast, drinking only water and fruit juices (but not too much citrus). Break your fast joyfully with another lunch.

2. The three-meal fast. If you've fasted before with good results, try a three-meal fast of about 30–36 hours—again drinking only fruit juice or water. Ideally, you would just pick a day and skip all meals (you might also alter other activities to concentrate on being with God).

3. The weekly two-meal or three-meal fast. A number of Christians fast on a weekly basis. Every Wednesday or every Friday (or any day) is a fasting day.

4. Longer options. Most experts do not recommend any fast longer than two or three meals, *unless you're an experienced faster.* If you know what you're doing, go for it. But make sure you consult your physician and a spiritual mentor or pastor. Your doctor can tell you how to make sure your body receives what's essential during your fast.

Breaking your fast. How you choose to break your fast is a very important health (and comfort) consideration. Start slowly with foods that are easy on your stomach (milk products are not recommended). Some people have found juices (not citrus), fruit (watermelon and cantaloupe), vegetables, and broth good for breaking fasts. And then gradually work back to your normal eating pattern.

NOTE: There are some people who should not fast: pregnant and post-pregnant women, diabetics, heart patients, and those with such conditions as gout, liver disease, kidney disease, cerebral disease, pulmonary problems, tumors, bleeding ulcers, cancer, and blood disease. If you have any medical or psychological condition, or if you are taking any regular medication, please consult your doctor first. For these people, we offer an alternative:

5. The replacement "fast." Find some other habit that is nearly as central to your life as food. Watching TV, playing computer games, surfing the net, talking on the phone, shopping. This does not have to be a bad habit (just as eating is not a bad thing), but it's something you will choose to give up for a certain period of time so you can focus on God in a special way.

Remember that the purpose of fasting is to "seek God"—to draw closer to him, putting him above your most basic needs. So use those hunger pangs and withdrawal symptoms to spark thoughts of God's presence. Take your normal eating time to pray, study Scripture, or to listen for God's still, small voice. Don't take pride in this as some major spiritual accomplishment, and don't push yourself beyond what God enables you to do. If you notice any unusual symptoms during your fast, use common sense or consult your physician. And avoid getting legalistic with yourself. Use this occasion to seek the Lord.

ASSIGNMENT OVERVIEW

For a full description of the action steps, see pages 8–17. This journal will give you daily reminders and weekly checkups to guide you through the assignments.

DAILY

1. Study the assigned Scripture passages and answer the questions in the journal.
2. Pray the Tension's Good Side Prayer, using the model on page 9.
3. On the chart on pages 40–41, list a way you've observed God ministering to or through you.

WEEKLY

1. Read the appropriate chapter in the Adventure Guidebook, *When the Troops Are Tired* (see below).
2. Pray for your pastor, especially in matters related to the sermon. Then make an effort to put your pastor's words into practice.
3. Memorize a Bible verse (see *The Tapped-Out Christian's Energy Pack*).

FIVE TIMES DURING THE ADVENTURE

1. Talk with someone about how God has ministered to or through you.

ONCE DURING THE ADVENTURE

1. Invite one or more people to join you for a simple time of Christian hospitality (see pp. 12–13).
2. Write your pastor a note telling how you've been influenced by the sermons and what issues you'd like to have addressed further (see pp. 14–15).
3. Practice a fast (see pp. 16–17).

Necessary Resources for This 50-Day Adventure

When the Troops Are Tired by David R. Mains (Adventure Guidebook or Audio Guidebook)

In addition to your journals, each household needs one copy of the Adventure Guidebook. Filled with motivational illustrations and practical helps, the eight chapters provide in-depth explanations of the Adventure themes. This book is an interesting and fast read that should enhance your 50-Day experience.

In *The Tapped-Out Christian's Energy Pack,* you'll find 23 revitalizing Bible verses you can use for memorization or meditation. This handy pack also contains the Tension's Good Side Prayer.

To order these resources, use the form on page 78 for convenient home delivery, or visit your church book table or local Christian bookstore.

WARM-UP
FRIDAY

UNTAPPED MIRACLES FOR TAPPED-OUT CHRISTIANS

Read Psalm 30.   **Date:**_____

1. Take a quick look at 1 Chronicles 21:1—22:6 to get an idea of what David had been going through when he wrote this psalm. List some of the emotions you believe David would have felt at the time.

_____

_____

2. David uses words like *depths, grave,* and *pit* (NIV). Do you relate to any of those? Why?

_____

3. What are some of the different things David says God has done for him recently? If you could choose one of those to be true in your case, what would it be?

_____

_____

_____

_____

4. Are verses 11–12 true of your life right now? What would you like to have happen during the next 51 days that would fill your heart with thanks to God?

_____

◇ *Read* the introductory material on pages 3–7.

◇ *Pray* the Tension's Good Side Prayer on page 9.

◇ *Read* the introduction in *When the Troops Are Tired* (see p. 18).

WARM-UP
SATURDAY

UNTAPPED MIRACLES FOR TAPPED-OUT CHRISTIANS

Read Acts 12:1–19.   **Date:**_____

1. Based on verses 1–5, what do you think the mood was among the believers?

_____

2. What was their response to this desperate situation?

_____

3. What does this passage imply about the importance of a Christian fellowship?

_____

4. How major a role does prayer play in your church?

_____

5. What is a miracle prayer request you have for your church as the Adventure begins?

_____

_____

_____

_____

◇ **Read** the action step descriptions on pages 8–17.

◇ **Pray** the Tension's Good Side Prayer on page 9.

◇ **Read** the introduction in *When the Troops Are Tired* (see p. 18).

LOOKING
BACK

MOVING
FORWARD

Check the box if you have completed the assignment.

◇ Read the introductory materials on pages 3–18.

◇ Read the introduction in the *When the Troops Are Tired* Guidebook.

◇ Completed the Warm-Up Days on pages 19–20.

Theme 1: Finding Tension's Good Side

Assignments for This Week:

◆ *Read* chapter 1 in *When the Troops Are Tired.*

◆ *Pray* for your pastor and the upcoming sermon.

◆ *Memorize* a verse (see The Tapped-Out Christian's Energy Pack).

Daily Assignments:

◆ *Read* the assigned Scripture passages and answer the questions.

◆ *Pray* the Tension's Good Side Prayer (see p. 9).

◆ *Write* down a way you've observed God ministering to or through you (pp. 40–41).

An Optional Resource for Adventure Theme 1:
Honestly by Sheila Walsh

The co-host of television's "700 Club," Sheila Walsh seemed to have it all. But her inner turmoils and fears brought on a pain too pressing to ignore, a pain that overwhelmed her completely. One morning she was on national television and by that night she was under psychiatric care—the first step in an intense personal pilgrimage back to emotional and spiritual health. A firsthand account, this book details the journey of a woman who thought she'd lost everything, only to find the good side to her suffering: a more honest and intimate relationship with Jesus.

To order this resource, use the form on page 78 for convenient home delivery, or visit your church book table or local Christian bookstore.

PRAY

Lord, when I understand that you can use even bad situations to bring glory to yourself, it's like tapping into a miracle. Give me faith to live believing that truth. Amen.

READ

Read Ruth 1:1–22; 4:13–17.

REFLECT

Under normal conditions you would have been granted tenure. But sometimes the academic community isn't tolerant of university faculty who live in a decidedly Christian manner. That's not fair, is it?

It's easier to live by faith when everything is going well, almost everyone likes you, and the world is fair. When that illusion is shattered, it's harder to hold on to the promises of God.

Often people get worn out when their tensions lead to dead ends. That's what happened to Naomi. She gave up on God, even suggesting that her hometown friends call her "Bitter." Bitter is what she felt God had made her life.

Ruth, on the other hand, appears to have believed that God would do what was best for her. She knew the same hardships as her mother-in-law. But she lived a life of quiet expectancy, and the Lord blessed her in ways far beyond anything she could ever have imagined.

APPLY

1. What difficult situations did Ruth and Naomi face?

_____

_____

2. When worn down by trials, do you tend to respond more like Ruth or Naomi?

_____

3. According to Ruth 4:13–17, what "miracles" did God bring about through the tensions of these women? What lessons can you learn from that?

_____

_____

PRAY

Pray the Tension's Good Side Prayer (p. 9).

1. What was the tension, or bad situation, occurring in Acts 8:1b–4?

_____

2. In what way did the godly people who were scattered find a good side to their tension? (See Acts 11:19–21.)

_____

3. What tensions might be wearing your church down presently?

_____

_____

_____

4. On page 9, you'll find the Tension's Good Side Prayer. Pray it on behalf of your church, using plural pronouns and inserting the tensions you listed above.

" WHY NOT LOOK AT THIS DIFFICULT TIME IN YOUR LIFE AS A CHANCE TO GROW SOME MORE?"

◇ *Pray* the Tension's Good Side Prayer on page 9.

◇ *Write* down a way you've observed God ministering to or through you on page 40.

◇ *Read* chapter 1 in *When the Troops Are Tired* (see p. 18).

DAY 3

1. What is a current difficulty in your life that wears you down? On a feeling level, how concerned do you perceive God to be about your problem?

_____

_____

2. James was writing to believers scattered by persecution. Why can Christians be joyful even when facing a situation that seems desperate (see verses 3–4)?

_____

_____

3. What do verses 5–8 say you can do if you need wisdom regarding your difficulty? How do these verses indicate you must pray?

_____

_____

4. The Tension's Good Side Prayer (p. 9) emphasizes that God is constantly working in your behalf. It encourages you to look for the joys of his miracle touch. Take a moment to pray the prayer with your difficulty in mind.

"Instead of insisting that God answer your requests for the church in the exact way you think he should, start looking for creative ways he might use what is happening to bring glory to himself."

David Mains, *When the Troops Are Tired,* page 14

◇ ***Pray*** the Tension's Good Side Prayer on page 9.

◇ ***Write*** down a way you've observed God ministering to or through you on page 40.

◇ ***Memorize*** a verse (see *The Tapped-Out Christian's Energy Pack* for suggestions).

1. Is there something in your past that still brings you shame and tension? What is it?

_____

2. How does Paul describe himself before Christ saved him? If that were your past, how would you feel about it?

_____

_____

3. What good came out of Paul's sinful past?

_____

4. Is there someone in your life for whom you'd like to see God do a miracle turnaround? How does knowing that God displayed patience and mercy to "the worst of sinners" (verse 16) encourage you?

_____

_"I spent a lot of time grieving over the picture of who I am without Christ. . . .
It may seem like a nightmare to face all that is true about ourselves, but
when we combine it with the glory of who we are in Christ, it is a gift
that will take us through the night until the morning breaks."_

Sheila Walsh, _Honestly,_ pages 209–210

◇ **Pray** the Tension's Good Side Prayer on page 9.

◇ **Write** down a way you've observed God ministering to or through you on page 40.

◇ **Read** chapter 1 in _When the Troops Are Tired._

1. What is a tension in your life you feel you can't resolve with the resources you have now?

_____

2. How big was Gideon's army when they started out? How big did it end up?

_____

3. Why did the Lord want to reduce the size of the army? What tension did that produce for Gideon and his men?

_____

_____

4. In this account, what is a miracle touch God provided for Gideon?

_____

5. What lesson might God want to teach you from this text?

_____

_____

_____

_____

◇ *Pray* the Tension's Good Side Prayer on page 9.

◇ *Write* down a way you've observed God ministering to or through you on page 40.

◇ *Pray* for your pastor and the upcoming sermon.

1. Dealing with a death of any kind is emotionally exhausting. How have you been affected by the death of a loved one? What about the death of a dream, a marriage, a business, or a church?

_____

_____

2. When Jesus received word that Lazarus was sick, why didn't he go straight to Bethany?

_____

3. What tensions were the disciples feeling? Mary and Martha? The onlookers? (See verses 16, 37.)

_____

_____

_____

4. Choose one or two of the people from Question 3. If they had had the Tension's Good Side Prayer available (p. 9), how do you suppose they would have responded to praying it, given their current tensions?

_____

_____

5. Now with new insight, pray the prayer as it relates to your own situation.

◇ *Write* down a way you've observed God ministering to or through you on page 40.

◇ *Read* chapter 1 in *When the Troops Are Tired.*

LOOKING
BACK

Check the box if you have completed the assignment.

◇ Completed Days 1–6.
◇ Prayed the Tension's Good Side Prayer.
◇ Prayed for my pastor.
◇ Wrote down ways I observed God ministering to or through me.
◇ Read chapter 1 in *When the Troops Are Tired.*
◇ Memorized a verse.

Optional Follow-Up Scriptures for Extra Study on Theme 1:

◆ Genesis 50:15–21
(see Genesis 37—50)
◆ Proverbs 3:5–6
◆ Acts 16:16–40
◆ 2 Corinthians 12:1–10

MOVING
FORWARD

Theme 2: The 24/7 Church

Assignments for This Week:

◆ *Read* chapter 2 in *When the Troops Are Tired.*
◆ *Pray* for your pastor and the upcoming sermon.
◆ *Memorize* a verse (see *The Tapped-Out Christian's Energy Pack*).

Daily Assignments:

◆ *Read* the assigned Scripture passages and answer the questions.
◆ *Pray* the Tension's Good Side Prayer (see p. 9).
◆ *Write* down a way you've observed God ministering to or through you (pp. 40–41).

Optional Resources for Adventure Theme 2:

Roaring Lambs by Bob Briner and the *Rack, Shack, and Benny* Veggie Tales Video

When it comes to influencing our culture, Emmy Award–winning TV producer Bob Briner thinks Christians are more like lambs than lions. In this empowering book, he explains why and how we can be 24/7 believers in the moral- and culture-shaping arenas of our society.

The *Rack, Shack, and Benny* Veggie Tales video is a fun way to explore Adventure Theme 2. Adults and children alike will love the original music and groundbreaking animation in this retelling of the biblical story of Shadrach, Meshach, and Abednego.

To order these resources, use the form on page 78 for convenient home delivery, or visit your church book table or local Christian bookstore.

PRAY

Lord, I love it when the church gathers. Help me to be as excited about the miracle of the church scattered throughout the week. Amen.

READ

Read Daniel, chapter 6.

REFLECT

It seldom feels uncomfortable or scary to attend a worship service. But living out your faith in the workplace is another matter. Having your minister encourage you to do that could feel like being fed to the lions.

Daniel was quite open about his daily walk with the Lord. He would have made any preacher proud. This high government official refused the efforts of his enemies to restrict his faith. The threat of being eaten alive only serves as a backdrop to the greatest miracle in the life of this hero, who chose to live out his faith every hour of every day.

Even today, a faith that's confined to an hour or so in church each weekend is not going to sufficiently energize believers for the rest of the week.

"Where's your church?" someone asked a friend.

"Depends on when you ask the question," was the response. "On Sunday mornings we meet in our sanctuary at Broadway and Archer. But come Monday, we straighten teeth, build homes, fly airplanes, type letters, wait tables, teach school . . . you name it." This person understood the Daniel mindset.

APPLY

1. When have you been in a Daniel-like situation where you were tempted not to pray in public because of outside pressures?

_____

2. As a 24/7 believer, what compromises might Daniel have considered to get around the king's edict?

_____

3. In verse 20, how does the king describe Daniel's service to God? Would someone who works or interacts with you on a regular basis describe you the same way? Why or why not?

_____

_____

_____

PRAY

Pray the Tension's Good Side Prayer.

1. Zacchaeus saw immediately that following Christ would affect every aspect of his life. He couldn't live one way on the Sabbath and another way during the week. What two things did he tell Jesus he would do?

_____

_____

2. What was Jesus' response to those two promises?

_____

3. In what way do you sense Christ may be challenging you, as a 24/7 Christian, to rethink how you relate your faith to your weekday activities?

_____

_____

4. What is one concrete step you could take this week? How might that energize your faith? Why not start today.

_____

_____

> "If we fill the air with praises to Jesus on 'his' day and hardly have time to think about him the other six days, if that kind of duplicity is more who we are than we care to admit, then it's no wonder our faith isn't all that alive. We're squandering energy attempting to juggle two different lifestyles."

David Mains, *When the Troops Are Tired*, page 25

◇ ***Pray*** the Tension's Good Side Prayer on page 9.

◇ ***Write*** down a way you've observed God ministering to or through you on page 40.

◇ ***Read*** chapter 2 in *When the Troops Are Tired*.

1. Use five adjectives to describe a modern-day version of the woman depicted in these verses.

_____

_____

2. List all the people who are affected by the daily work of the wife of noble character.

_____

_____

3. From these verses, what indicates that this was a woman of faith?

_____

4. Name a Christian woman you're aware of who shares many of the qualities of this Proverbs 31 woman. (You might consider sending her a note or giving her a call.)

_____

5. What is one quality you'd like to adopt as you seek to be a 24/7 believer?

_____

_____

> *"Keeping Christ bottled up in the churches is keeping salt in the shakers, and He does not go where we do not take Him. We need to take Him everywhere . . . and show His relevance to every aspect of modern life."*

Bob Briner, *Roaring Lambs,* page 38

◇ **Pray** the Tension's Good Side Prayer on page 9.

◇ **Write** down a way you've observed God ministering to or through you on page 40.

◇ **Talk** with someone about how God has ministered to or through you.

1. What influences play a major part in how you live your day-to-day life (TV, friends, family, newspaper, and so on)?

_____

_____

2. In the course of an average week, how often are you conscious of God's Word as an influence in how you live?

_____

3. In this passage, why does Moses say God is giving his commandments to the nation of Israel?

_____

_____

4. In what ways are the instructions of verses 6–8 similar to or at odds with your current lifestyle?

_____

_____

5. What are some of the activities in your everyday routine that could be transformed into time with God (commuting to work, exercise times, doing household chores, waiting for others)?

_____

_____

◇ *Pray* the Tension's Good Side Prayer on page 9.

◇ *Write* down a way you've observed God ministering to or through you on page 40.

◇ *Read* chapter 2 in *When the Troops Are Tired.*

Note: In this passage Paul is addressing a current practice that was the result of hardness of heart. He is not approving of slavery.

1. People often think of serving God as an activity that happens primarily at church. Does this passage seem to support that understanding? Why or why not?

_____

_____

2. Summarize in your own words the principle of this passage regarding everyday work and service to God.

_____

_____

3. In what ways do you do your everyday tasks in agreement with verses 7–8? In what ways are your actions in disagreement?

_____

_____

4. How might your life seem miraculously different if you attempted to serve God instead of humans in all things?

_____

_____

◇ *Pray* the Tension's Good Side Prayer on page 9.

◇ *Write* down a way you've observed God ministering to or through you on page 40.

◇ *Memorize* a verse (see *The Tapped-Out Christian's Energy Pack*).

FRIDAY   DATE

THEME 2 THE 24/7 CHURCH

READ COLOSSIANS 4:2–6

1. Is Paul talking about church activities or everyday activities? What clues are there in the passage to guide you in your answer?

_____

_____

2. How does Paul, although in prison, hope to impact non-Christians? How does he encourage the Colossian believers to be impacting non-Christians?

_____

_____

3. What are some activities in your life that you really enjoy, which you could "make the most of" in behalf of nonbelievers?

_____

_____

4. List some of the nonbelievers you come in contact with on a regular basis. Take some time to prayerfully consider how you could make the most of your time with them.

_____

_____

5. How has recording the ways God has spoken to and through you (see p. 40) helped you be more aware of your role as a 24/7 believer?

_____

_____

◇ *Pray* the Tension's Good Side Prayer on page 9.

◇ *Write* down a way you've observed God ministering to or through you on page 40.

◇ *Pray* for your pastor and the upcoming sermon.

LOOKING
BACK

Check the box if you have completed the assignment.

◇ Completed Days 7–13.

◇ Prayed the Tension's Good Side Prayer.

◇ Prayed for my pastor.

◇ Wrote down ways I observed God ministering to or through me.

◇ Read chapter 2 in *When the Troops Are Tired.*

◇ Memorized a verse.

Optional Follow-Up Scriptures for Extra Study on Theme 2:

◆ Daniel 3:1–30

◆ Colossians 3:23–24

◆ 1 Peter 2:11–12

◆ 1 Peter 3:13–16

MOVING
FORWARD

Theme 3: Christian Hospitality

Assignments for This Week:

◆ **Read** chapter 3 in *When the Troops Are Tired.*

◆ **Pray** for your pastor and the upcoming sermon.

◆ **Talk** with someone about how God has ministered to or through you.

◆ **Memorize** a verse.

Before the Adventure Is Over (Do Once):

◆ **Invite** one or more people to join you for a simple time of Christian hospitality (see pp. 12–13).

Daily Assignments:

◆ **Read** the assigned Scripture passages and answer the questions.

◆ **Pray** the Tension's Good Side Prayer.

◆ **Write** down a way you've observed God ministering to or through you.

An Optional Resource for Adventure Theme 3:
Open Heart, Open Home by Karen Mains

In this inhospitable world, a Christian home is truly a miracle to be shared. Unfortunately, too many North American believers, immobilized by our culture's emphasis on entertainment, avoid extending the healing hand of Christian hospitality. This life-changing book provides biblical principles and practical helps for opening your heart and home— whether you live in a country farm house, a condo in the suburbs, or a walk-up apartment in the city.

To order this resource, use the form on page 78 for convenient home delivery, or visit your church book table or local Christian bookstore.

PRAY

Lord, teach me the joys of using my home as a ministry base. I'm not sure I know how to do that, but I'm willing to learn. Amen.

READ

Read Luke 10:38–42.

REFLECT

People in New Testament times didn't have last names. But the Martha in this passage sounds like she could have been related to the famous entertainment expert of our day, Martha Stewart. "Distracted by all the preparations that had to be made," the biblical Martha needed to learn that hospitality begins with people and their needs. Jesus said Martha was worried and upset about many things. According to our Lord, Mary had chosen a better way.

When Christian hospitality again marks the church, the sanctuary no longer will be thought of as the primary place for ministry. That should be exciting to most men and women because they feel more comfortable in their own surroundings, especially when they don't try to be pretentious.

In this inhospitable world, Christian homes are miracles to be shared. But we can't fall into the trap of copying what the world emphasizes when it does its entertaining.

APPLY

1. Do you tend to be more like Mary or Martha when you open your home to others? Why?

_____

_____

2. Based on this passage, what characterizes true hospitality?

_____

3. Read Action Step 3 (p. 12) to review how you can show true hospitality during this Adventure.

PRAY

Pray the Tension's Good Side Prayer.

1. Name a time when you were shown Christian hospitality. How did that treatment make you feel?

_____

2. Based on these two passages, who in a church is responsible for hospitality?

_____

3. How does the fact that both leaders and parishioners were encouraged to serve others hospitably challenge your thinking about hospitality?

_____

_____

4. Do you need help to complete Action Step 3 (p. 12)? If so, who could help you?

_____

5. Might you be able to help someone else carry out Action Step 3? Who?

_____

"I've found the key is not so much opening your home (even though that's very important) as it is opening your heart. . . . This kind of open-heart hospitality can be given whether you're sitting on the floor and eating with your fingers or moving boxes of papers off the table to make room for the carry-out bags."

David Mains, *When the Troops Are Tired*, page 46

◇ *Pray* the Tension's Good Side Prayer on page 9.

◇ *Write* down a way you've observed God ministering to or through you on page 40.

◇ *Read* chapter 3 in *When the Troops Are Tired*.

1. List all the things Peter instructs his readers to do in this passage.

_____

_____

_____

2. Are you surprised to find the idea of hospitality in such a list? Why or why not?

_____

3. How does Peter instruct us to practice hospitality? What might this mean in a practical sense as you invite others to your home?

_____

4. Who is someone you know who needs to experience true Christian love and hospitality?

_____

5. How might you be able to put both verses 8 and 9 into practice at once? What plans can you be making now to do that?

_____

_____

◇ *Pray* the Tension's Good Side Prayer on page 9.

◇ *Write* down a way you've observed God ministering to or through you on page 40.

◇ *Invite* one or more people to join you for a simple time of Christian hospitality.

1. Based on this passage, how would you describe Nabal? What in particular leads you to think so?

_____

2. How is Abigail different from Nabal? What clues do you find about her character in the story?

_____

_____

3. What does Abigail do when she learns of her husband's lack of hospitality toward David and his men? What events unfold as a result of her generosity?

_____

_____

_____

4. Can you recall a time when hospitality improved a relationship? Describe what happened.

_____

_____

5. What kind of guidance does Abigail's example give you? Has there been, or is there now, a situation in your life that could be improved with some hospitality? When could you make that happen?

_____

_____

◇ *Pray* the Tension's Good Side Prayer on page 9.

◇ *Write* down a way you've observed God ministering to or through you on page 40.

◇ *Pray* for your pastor and the upcoming sermon.

The Three T's: To, Through, and Talk About

In the spaces provided, record a way God has ministered *to* you or *through* you. Then, five times during the Adventure, *talk about* one of these experiences with someone. For more information on Action Step 2 and being a 24/7 believer, see page 10.

DAY 1

DAY 2

DAY 3

DAY 4

DAY 5

DAY 6

DAY 7

DAY 8

DAY 9

DAY 10

DAY 11

DAY 12

DAY 13

DAY 14

DAY 15

DAY 16

DAY 17

DAY 18

DAY 19

DAY 20

DAY 21

DAY 22

DAY 23

DAY 24

DAY 25

DAY 26

DAY 27

DAY 28

DAY 29

DAY 30

DAY 31

DAY 32

DAY 33

DAY 34

DAY 35

DAY 36

DAY 37

DAY 38

DAY 39

DAY 40

DAY 41

DAY 42

DAY 43

DAY 44

DAY 45

DAY 46

DAY 47

DAY 48

DAY 49

DAY 50

1. What happens to those who give to others freely? What happens to those who do not?

_____

_____

2. Can you recall a time when you gave freely to others? What did you do?

3. What happened to others as a result of your actions? What happened to you?

_____

_____

4. Refreshing others can sound exhausting. In what specific ways could you be refreshed by refreshing others?

_____

_____

5. Believers are energized when they make meaningful connections. In what ways is it easier to do that in a home setting than in a church setting?

_____

_____

◇ **Pray** the Tension's Good Side Prayer on page 9.

◇ **Write** down a way you've observed God ministering to or through you on page 40.

◇ **Memorize** a verse (see _The Tapped-Out Christian's Energy Pack_).

1. What three things does this passage command the Hebrew believers to do?

_____

_____

2. Do you think you would be drawn to a church community that did those things? Why or why not?

_____

3. In verse 2, what is the writer's point about entertaining angels?

_____

_____

4. How can you expand your thinking about hospitality to include strangers and those in prison?

_____

_____

5. How are you progressing with Action Step 3 (p. 12)?

_____

> *"Can we learn to live as adventurously as Christ? Can we discover that hospitality is not what we have, but what we are?"*
>
> Karen Mains, *Open Heart, Open Home,* page 196

◇ *Pray* the Tension's Good Side Prayer on page 9.

◇ *Write* down a way you've observed God ministering to or through you on page 40.

◇ *Read* chapter 3 in *When the Troops Are Tired.*

LOOKING BACK

Check the box if you have completed the assignment.

◇ Completed Days 14–20.
◇ Prayed the Tension's Good Side Prayer.
◇ Prayed for my pastor.
◇ Wrote down ways I observed God ministering to or through me.
◇ Read chapter 3 in *When the Troops Are Tired*.
◇ Memorized a verse.

Optional Follow-Up Scriptures for Extra Study on Theme 3:

◆ Genesis 8:1–16
◆ Luke 7:36–50
◆ Luke 14:1–14
◆ Acts 16:11–15
 (See also vv. 16–40.)

MOVING FORWARD

Theme 4: Pulpit/Pew Mutual Support

Assignments for This Week:

◆ *Read* chapter 4 in *When the Troops Are Tired*.
◆ *Pray* for your pastor and the upcoming sermon.
◆ *Talk* with someone about how God has ministered to or through you.
◆ *Memorize* a verse.

Before the Adventure Is Over (Do Once):

◆ *Invite* one or more people for a time of Christian hospitality.
◆ *Write* a note to your pastor (see pp. 14–15).

Daily Assignments:

◆ *Read* the assigned Scripture passages and answer the questions.
◆ *Pray* the Tension's Good Side Prayer.
◆ *Write* down a way you've observed God ministering to or through you.

An Optional Resource for Adventure Theme 4:

Partners in Prayer by John Maxwell

Busy at the office of his new church, Pastor John Maxwell's morning was interrupted by a visit from an older man he'd never met. "John, the reason I came here today is so that I could pray for you." Maxwell knew immediately that God's agenda was taking over his own. Fourteen years later the results are unmistakably evident in his growing and vibrant congregation. The author explains how you, too, can unleash the potential of committed prayer support for your pastor and your church.

 To order this resource, use the form on page 78 for convenient home delivery, or visit your church book table or local Christian bookstore.

PRAY
Lord, I want the picture of Aaron and Hur supporting the hands of Moses to reflect how our pastor and parishioners work together. Amen.

READ
Read Exodus 17:8–13.

REFLECT
Interesting and inspiring sermons are always appreciated. Uninteresting and uninspiring sermons wear people out. They're hard on pastors and parishioners alike. With so much riding on these key weekly presentations, it's surprising how few people are actively involved in some kind of supportive role.

Most ministers feel they don't receive enough constructive feedback about their messages. They also question whether their people are faithfully supporting them in prayer.

Parishioners aren't sure their input or response is always wanted. If it is, how should they make their thoughts known? And how should they pray for their pastor's sermon preparation and delivery?

Unfortunately, the enemy wins when issues like these go unresolved. During this Spiritual Adventure you'll find some suggestions that can be beneficial to both pastors and parishioners. As you learn to better support your minister, keep in mind this Old Testament picture of Moses' hands being held high by Aaron and Hur.

APPLY
1. What in this account appeals to you?

_____

2. Do you identify most with Moses, Aaron, or Hur? Why?

_____

3. What is one way you can make this picture a reality in your congregation?

_____

PRAY
Pray the Tension's Good Side Prayer.

1. Have you ever wished you could ask a question about something said during a sermon? How do you respond to Christ's allowing the Pharisees to question what he was saying?

_____

_____

2. If someone friendly toward your church wanted to ask questions, what opportunities would there be?

_____

_____

3. If someone outside the church were antagonistic toward Christ but wanted to ask honest questions, what forum might your church provide?

_____

4. As the Son of God, Jesus always knew what people were thinking. How do you suppose present-day pastors get a handle on how people are responding to their preaching and teaching?

_____

_____

"If a service is boring, I want to know why so I can work to make it more interesting. If my sermon isn't touching people where they live, it only makes sense that they have a constructive way to make suggestions for improvement."

David Mains, *When the Troops Are Tired*, pages 63–64

◇ **Pray** the Tension's Good Side Prayer on page 9.

◇ **Write** down a way you've observed God ministering to or through you on page 40.

◇ **Read** chapter 4 in *When the Troops Are Tired*.

1. Based on verses 3, 6, and 9, list all the things the Israelites did.

_____

_____

_____

2. Based on verses 3, 7–9, list all the things Ezra and the priests did.

_____

_____

3. In verses 9–12, what is the range of emotions the people experienced?

_____

_____

4. Can you recall a time in your church or elsewhere when the people responded emotionally to hearing God's Word? Describe the experience.

_____

_____

5. How can you prepare yourself to be open to the Spirit's moving when you hear the Word preached? Might your pastor benefit from knowing your response?

_____

_____

◇ **Pray** the Tension's Good Side Prayer on page 9.

◇ **Write** down a way you've observed God ministering to or through you on page 41.

◇ **Memorize** a verse (see *The Tapped-Out Christian's Energy Pack*).

1. What specific prayer requests is Paul making in verses 1–2?

_____

_____

2. In what ways are present-day ministers under attack from the evil one?

_____

_____

3. What can keep you from praying effectively for your pastor?

_____

_____

4. What is one step you could take to begin to overcome those obstacles?

_____

5. How do you think your church might change if all the members regularly prayed for your pastor?

_____

_____

> *"God's hand moves when people and pastors pray together.*
> *Through prayer, God makes the impossible, possible."*

John Maxwell, *Partners in Prayer,* page 7

◇ ***Pray*** the Tension's Good Side Prayer on page 9.

◇ ***Write*** down a way you've observed God ministering to or through you on page 41.

◇ ***Invite*** one or more people to join you for a simple time of Christian hospitality.

1. This passage is the conclusion of the well-known Sermon on the Mount (chapters 5–7). Given that context, when Jesus says "these words of mine" (verse 24), what is he talking about?

_____

2. Who does Jesus describe as being wise? Who does he describe as being foolish?

_____

3. Quickly review chapters 5–7. What is one teaching you have difficulty putting into practice?

_____

4. Is your difficulty because you refuse to obey or because you don't know how to put the teaching (such as "do not worry") into practice?

_____

5. Action Step 4 (p. 14) encourages you to write a supportive note to your pastor. Is your answer for Question 3 an area with which you could use some help through a sermon or teaching? Why not mention it in your note.

◇ *Pray* the Tension's Good Side Prayer on page 9.

◇ *Write* down a way you've observed God ministering to or through you on page 41.

◇ *Talk* with someone about how God has ministered to or through you.

◇ *Pray* for and write a note to your pastor (see pp. 14–15).

1. From verse 12, what was the result of the Bereans' interaction with Paul's preaching?

_____

_____

2. If you were responsible for the spiritual growth of a congregation, how do you think a Berean attitude among them would help you in your ministry?

_____

_____

3. In verses 16–34, Paul is open to the questions of his hearers. What are some questions you have about Scripture and how it applies to your life?

_____

_____

_____

_____

4. Have you written a note to your pastor for Action Step 4 (p. 14)? If not, which of the questions you just listed might you offer in your note as a possible sermon or teaching topic?

_____

_____

◇ *Pray* the Tension's Good Side Prayer on page 9.

◇ *Write* down a way you've observed God ministering to or through you on page 41.

◇ *Read* chapter 4 in *When the Troops Are Tired.*

LOOKING
BACK

MOVING
FORWARD

Check the box if you have completed the assignment.

◇ Completed Days 21–27.

◇ Prayed the Tension's Good Side Prayer.

◇ Prayed for my pastor.

◇ Wrote down ways I observed God ministering to or through me.

◇ Read chapter 4 in *When the Troops Are Tired.*

◇ Memorized a verse.

Optional Follow-Up Scriptures for Extra Study on Theme 4:

◆ Romans 15:30–33

◆ Ephesians 6:10–20

◆ Philippians 1:1–11

◆ James 1:22–25

Theme 5: Prayer with Fasting

Assignments for This Week:

◆ *Read* chapter 5 in *When the Troops Are Tired.*

◆ *Talk* with someone about how God has ministered to or through you.

◆ *Memorize* a verse.

Before the Adventure Is Over (Do Once):

◆ *Practice* a fast (see pp. 16–17).

◆ *Invite* one or more people for a time of Christian hospitality.

◆ *Write* your pastor a note (see pp. 14–15).

Daily Assignments:

◆ *Read* the assigned Scripture passages and answer the questions.

◆ *Write* down a way you've observed God ministering to or through you.

◆ *Pray* the Tension's Good Side Prayer.

An Optional Resource for Adventure Theme 5:
The Coming Revival by Bill Bright

Surely our nation needs a visit from our great God in heaven. Respected international Christian leader Bill Bright is convinced it's coming—but only after fervent prayer and fasting by millions of God's people. This highly acclaimed book describes North America's desperate need for spiritual revival and how God is calling us to repent, fast, and pray. Recounting his own experience with fasting, the author also provides practical insights to help you prepare for and undertake prayer with fasting.

To order this resource, use the form on page 78 for convenient home delivery, or visit your church book table or local Christian bookstore.

PRAY

Lord, most of your children feel like novices when it comes to disciplines such as fasting. Our baby steps of faith need your steadying presence. Thank you. Amen.

READ

Read Esther 4:12–17.

REFLECT

Almost everyone knows what it's like to be in a situation where you desperately need help and you need it fast. If friends come to your rescue, you're forever grateful.

Esther knew she was facing something beyond her ability to resolve. She not only needed friends, she needed the Lord to intervene. But she was aware of a miracle resource to which she could turn. After a three-day fast by all of God's people, the Lord won the day.

In the past few decades, we have seen the fire power of the enemy increase greatly. It's time for God's people to look for additional resources to use in the battle. Many Christian leaders believe that prayer with fasting is a spiritual weapon that needs to be rediscovered. It certainly worked in Esther's situation.

Could prayer with fasting be one of the untapped "miracles" God is encouraging his people to rediscover today?

APPLY

1. What events led up to Esther's decision to fast and ask others to join her (see Esther 3:12—4:10)?

_____

_____

2. What present situation in your life might benefit from the untapped "miracle" of fasting?

_____

3. In what ways is Esther's response similar to or different from your own response to adversity? What from Esther's example encourages or challenges you?

_____

PRAY

Pray the Tension's Good Side Prayer.

DAY 30

MONDAY   DATE

THEME 5 PRAYER WITH FASTING
READ MATTHEW 4:1–11

1. How did Jesus prepare for his upcoming confrontation with the devil?

_____

_____

2. How does verse 3 describe Satan? What three things does Satan tempt Jesus with in this passage?

_____

_____

3. If you were writing an article on the outcome of Jesus' struggle with Satan, what would be your heading?

_____

_____

4. How does this passage challenge you to prepare for times of spiritual testing? Is there such a time in your life presently?

_____

_____

5. In light of Jesus' example, what is your response to Action Step 5 (review pp. 16–17)?

_____

"[John Wesley] said, 'Some have exalted religious fasting beyond all Scripture and reason; and others have utterly disregarded it.' Do you find yourself at one of those extremes?"

David Mains, *When the Troops Are Tired*, page 91

◇ **Pray** the Tension's Good Side Prayer on page 9.

◇ **Write** down a way you've observed God ministering to or through you on page 41.

◇ **Read** chapter 5 in *When the Troops Are Tired*.

1. Why does Ezra proclaim a fast for those returning to Jerusalem with him from exile? What besides fasting does Ezra's group do (see verse 23)?

_____

_____

2. Why didn't Ezra want to ask the king for help? How do you think the king would have viewed Ezra and his God if he had been asked to help protect the returning exiles?

_____

_____

3. What were the exciting results of Ezra's prayer with fasting? (Read the rest of chapter 8.)

_____

_____

4. Are you in need of God's protection in a given area? If so, what does this passage say to you?

_____

5. How can you follow Ezra's example in the future when you are concerned about representing God well?

_____

_____

◇ *Pray* the Tension's Good Side Prayer on page 9.

◇ *Write* down a way you've observed God ministering to or through you on page 41.

◇ *Practice* a fast (see pp. 16–17).

1. According to these verses, whose attention should you be seeking when praying and fasting? What reward will those who publicly draw attention to their praying and fasting receive?

_____

_____

2. What do Jesus' admonitions against attracting attention to oneself through prayer and fasting tell you about seeking human approval in your spirituality?

_____

_____

3. Jesus is encouraging us to move beyond mere appearances of spirituality to openly and honestly come to God. Do you think that generally characterizes your spiritual life? When are some times you have wanted to appear spiritual so others would not think less of you?

_____

_____

4. What does this passage say to you regarding Action Step 5 (pp. 16–17)?

_____

> *"Not only will fasting and prayer transform an individual or church, it can change the course of a nation."*
>
> Bill Bright, *The Coming Revival,* page 102

◇ **Pray** the Tension's Good Side Prayer on page 9.

◇ **Write** down a way you've observed God ministering to or through you on page 41.

◇ **Invite** one or more people for a time of Christian hospitality.

DAY 33

1. Reread verses 12–13, picturing yourself in this situation. What are your feelings?

_____

_____

2. Review the passage and list all the things Jehoshaphat and the nation do in response to the news of imminent invasion.

_____

_____

_____

3. When recently have you felt you needed to seek the Lord in a special way? Which of the things you listed for Question 2 have you participated in? Which of them tend to get overlooked? Why do you think that happens?

_____

_____

_____

4. From this passage, do you get the sense that fasting was a form of self-denial for its own sake? Or was it a way of concentrating more fully on seeking God? How does this passage impact your concept of fasting?

_____

_____

◇ **Pray** the Tension's Good Side Prayer on page 9.

◇ **Write** down a way you've observed God ministering to or through you on page 41.

◇ **Read** chapter 5 in *When the Troops Are Tired*.

◇ **Memorize** a verse (see *The Tapped-Out Christian's Energy Pack*).

FRIDAY   DATE

THEME 5 PRAYER WITH FASTING

READ ACTS 13:1–3

1. According to verse 2, what were the believers at Antioch doing when the Spirit called Barnabas and Saul? From this verse how often, does it seem, was fasting a part of their activities? Support your answer.

_____

_____

2. What four activities—responses to the Spirit's calling of Saul and Barnabas—are listed in verse 3?

_____

_____

3. These verses indicate that the early church regularly engaged in fasting, especially when dealing with important issues or seeking God's direction. What are some important issues facing your congregation?

_____

_____

4. Based on the example of the believers in Antioch, how frequently do you think fasting should be considered as you deal with your current concerns?

_____

5. What might be some spiritual benefits of fasting for you or your church?

_____

_____

◇ *Pray* the Tension's Good Side Prayer on page 9.

◇ *Write* down a way you've observed God ministering to or through you on page 41.

◇ *Practice* a fast (see pp. 16–17).

LOOKING
BACK

MOVING
FORWARD

Check the box if you have completed the assignment.
◇ Completed Days 28–34.
◇ Prayed the Tension's Good Side Prayer.
◇ Wrote down ways I observed God ministering to or through me.
◇ Read chapter 5 in *When the Troops Are Tired*.
◇ Memorized a verse.

Optional Follow-Up Scriptures for Extra Study on Theme 5:
◆ Deuteronomy 9:7–21
◆ Isaiah 58:1–14
◆ Joel 2:12–19
◆ Jonah 3:1–10

Theme 6: Telling Our Stories

Assignments for This Week:
◆ *Read* chapter 6 in *When the Troops Are Tired*.
◆ *Talk* with someone about how God has ministered to or through you.
◆ *Memorize* a verse.

Before the Adventure Is Over (Do Once):
◆ *Practice* a fast (see pp. 16–17).
◆ *Invite* one or more people for a time of Christian hospitality.
◆ *Write* your pastor a note.

Daily Assignments:
◆ *Read* the assigned Scripture passages and answer the questions.
◆ *Pray* the Tension's Good Side Prayer.
◆ *Write* down a way you've observed God ministering to or through you.

An Optional Resource for Adventure Theme 6:
The Power of Story by Leighton Ford

It's the oldest, purest, most natural way to reach people for Jesus Christ—by telling the great Story of God's grace. So why have so many Christians forgotten how to use this effective tool? This compelling book, written by inter-national evangelist Dr. Leighton Ford, explains how you can experience the joy of leading others to Christ—simply by telling them the story of how God has impacted your life.

To order this resource, use the form on page 78 for convenient home delivery, or visit your church book table or local Christian bookstore.

PRAY

Lord, all of us have personal stories to tell. The best ones show how our story and your story connect. Thank you for making that possible. Amen.

....

READ

Read Joshua 1:1–9.

....

REFLECT

"If you go with me, I'll do it." That thought has been expressed time and again. When a friend goes through an intimidating experience with us, we feel more secure.

At the office cafeteria it's harder to pray over a meal when we're by ourselves than it is when we're with a Christian friend. Similarly, it's better to hear how someone else has handled a difficult situation than to think we're the first Christian in the history of the world to experience a given tension.

That's why it's extremely important for us to share stories related to our everyday walk of faith. Doing so encourages both those who hear and those who tell. Stories help us to be all that God intended each day.

Joshua had a huge new responsibility on his shoulders. But the Lord had granted him the privilege of watching how Moses handled the pressure. With first-hand knowledge of Moses' story, Joshua could now be encouraged as he lived out the sequel to the Exodus.

....

APPLY

1. God referred to the example of Moses as he tried to allay Joshua's fears. What promise did God give Joshua that related to the story of Moses?

_____

2. Who is someone whose faith story has encouraged you?

_____

3. If someone asked about your story, what is a recent spiritual lesson God has taught you that you could share?

_____

_____

....

PRAY

Pray the Tension's Good Side Prayer.

1. List several things this psalm is calling the reader to do. Based on verses 1–4, what emotions do you sense the author felt when writing this psalm?

_____

_____

_____

2. Why does the psalmist recount stories? (See the end of the chapter for a clue.)

_____

3. If you wrote a psalm like this, what are two or three personal faith stories you'd include?

_____

_____

4. If you wrote a psalm about your church's faith stories, which ones would you select?

_____

_____

5. Stories about how God has worked in your life result in praise to God. What is an event you could share with someone to bring praise to God and encouragement to those who hear?

_____

◇ *Pray* the Tension's Good Side Prayer on page 9.

◇ *Write* down a way you've observed God ministering to or through you on page 41.

◇ *Read* chapter 6 in *When the Troops Are Tired*.

1. How many times in this passage does the blind man tell his story about Jesus healing his sight? To whom does he tell his story?

_____

2. When the blind man was questioned by the Pharisees, what did he keep telling them? How did they react?

_____

_____

3. What reactions have you received from people when you tell stories of how God has worked in your life?

_____

4. Have you ever shared a story with someone who questioned whether it was really true or whether it was God who brought it about? How did that affect your perspective on the experience?

_____

5. On a scale of 1 to 10, 10 being very often and 1 being very little, where do you place yourself with regard to telling your faith stories? Would you like that to change? If so, how?

_____

> *"It's almost impossible not to listen to someone who begins what he or she has to say with, 'Let me share something unusual that happened . . .'"*

David Mains, *When the Troops Are Tired,* page 106

◇ *Pray* the Tension's Good Side Prayer on page 9.

◇ *Write* down a way you've observed God ministering to or through you on page 41.

◇ *Memorize* a verse (see *The Tapped-Out Christian's Energy Pack*).

1. Would you describe Paul's defense before Agrippa as more of a legal argument or a retelling of the events of Paul's life?

_____

2. Based on verses 1b and 29, Paul obviously wanted two things to happen as a result of telling his story. What were they?

_____

_____

3. From verses 28–32, did Paul succeed in defending himself before Agrippa? Did he succeed in converting Agrippa to Christianity?

_____

4. Since Paul could have been put to death by Agrippa, what does this say about Paul's desire to tell the story of how Christ had redeemed him? How does Paul's example challenge or encourage you?

_____

_____

5. What was Festus' response to Paul in verse 24? Has someone ever responded in a similar manner to you? What can you learn from Paul's example?

_____

_____

◇ **Pray** the Tension's Good Side Prayer on page 9.

◇ **Write** down a way you've observed God ministering to or through you on page 41.

◇ **Talk** with someone about how God has ministered to or through you.

1. How long was the Feast of Tabernacles? What were the people to present to God during this time? Where were the people to live?

_____

_____

2. What was the reason for their giving offerings and living in tents?

_____

3. If you were an ancient Israelite, how do you think the duration, activities, and accommodation arrangements would affect you? Do you believe you or your descendants would easily forget God's deliverance from Egypt? Why or why not?

_____

_____

4. What are some of the special things you do in your church or family that remind you of God's provision? How do those activities help you hand down the faith?

_____

_____

5. How can you personally get away from your normal routine to renew your identity as a child of God (short retreat, Promise Keepers, and so forth)?

_____

_____

◇ **Pray** the Tension's Good Side Prayer on page 9.

◇ **Write** down a way you've observed God ministering to or through you on page 41.

◇ **Read** chapter 6 in *When the Troops Are Tired*.

1. Deborah and Barak wrote a song to commemorate the defeat of Sisera and his army (Judges 4). What apparently was their motivation for doing so?

_____

2. If you wrote a song about God's working in your life, what would you not want to leave out?

_____

3. What would be the tone of your song? Grateful? Worshipful? Joyful? Contemplative?

_____

4. What are some ways you can preserve your personal or family faith stories (such as keeping a diary or scrapbook)?

_____

_____

5. What would be the theme of a song you'd love to be able to write a year from now?

_____

> *"If you have become a part of the Story of God, then you have a story to share with the people around you."*
>
> Leighton Ford, *The Power of Story,* page 15

◇ **Pray** the Tension's Good Side Prayer on page 9.

◇ **Write** down a way you've observed God ministering to or through you on page 41.

◇ **Invite** one or more people for a time of Christian hospitality.

◇ **Pray** for and write your pastor a note (see pp. 14–15).

LOOKING
BACK

Check the box if you have completed the assignment.

◇ Completed Days 35–41.
◇ Prayed the Tension's Good Side Prayer.
◇ Wrote down ways I observed God ministering to or through me.
◇ Read chapter 6 in *When the Troops Are Tired*.
◇ Memorized a verse.

Optional Follow-Up Scriptures for Extra Study on Theme 6:

◆ Exodus 12:1–28
◆ Psalm 77
◆ Psalm 78:1–4
◆ 2 Peter 1:1–21

MOVING
FORWARD

Theme 7: The Wider Kingship
Theme 8: The Living Christ

Assignments for This Week:

◆ *Read* chapters 7–8 in *When the Troops Are Tired*.
◆ *Talk* with someone about how God has ministered to or through you.
◆ *Memorize* a verse.

Complete the Following:

◆ *Invite* one or more people for a time of Christian hospitality.
◆ *Write* your pastor a note.
◆ *Practice* a fast (see pp. 16–17).

Daily Assignments:

◆ *Read* the assigned Scripture passages and answer the questions.
◆ *Write* down ways you've observed God ministering to or through you.
◆ *Pray* the Tension's Good Side Prayer.

An Optional Resource for Adventure Themes 7 and 8:
The Body by Charles Colson

The true church is not a building. Nor is it just a collection of people. It's a worldwide community of believers whose Head is Jesus Christ. In this thought-provoking book, Chuck Colson uses a myriad of illustrations from around the world to paint a stirring picture of Christ's "wider kingship." You'll feel more connected to this greater church, which includes all races, colors, backgrounds, and corners of the globe.

To order this resource, use the form on page 78 for convenient home delivery, or visit your church book table or local Christian bookstore.

PRAY

Lord, not everyone who walks in the truth attends our church. Please help me get to know some of those fellow believers. Amen.

READ

Read 3 John.

REFLECT

Fighting within the ranks causes Christians to be tapped out. That's true for congregations, denominations, and the church worldwide. Believers agree on more than we disagree on. What a miracle it would be if we could learn to better work together.

Quite frequently, "spiritual" differences are really personality conflicts in disguise. That certainly was the case with Diotrephes. According to John, there was a hidden reason why Diotrephes wasn't more cooperative. He loved to be first. How embarrassing to be exposed like that for all time, and by the apostle closest to our Lord.

This short letter underscores that it's important to walk in the truth. Throughout history, a great deal of energy rightly has been expended as Christians have spelled out what they believe and why churches are not all the same. Maybe it would be more expedient now, however, for believers to start concentrating on what we hold in common.

APPLY

1. List several ways Diotrephes was damaging the church.

_____

_____

2. Diotrephes had a narrow view of who could be included in the church. Demetrius, Gaius, and John were more expansive in their thinking. Have your views expanded about who should be included in the family of God? If so, how?

_____

3. What is a lesson you've learned by reading or interacting with someone from a Christian tradition other than your own?

_____

PRAY

Pray the Tension's Good Side Prayer.

1. What is happening in verses 12–17? What does Rehoboam do to help bring about this splitting of the northern Israel (ten tribes) and the southern Judah (two tribes)?

_____

_____

2. In 11:1, how does Rehoboam intend to unite the northern part of the kingdom with the southern part, which he still rules?

_____

3. What is God's response to the idea of his people fighting one another?

_____

4. What are situations you're aware of where God's people have literally warred against each other?

_____

5. When in your life have you been too quick to enter into conflict with another believer? How might you have handled the situation differently?

_____

_____

"Fortunately, it's not necessary to come to a final conclusion on which churches are 'kosher' and which ones aren't in order to network better. . . . Once we [reach out a little], instead of feeling the exhaustion of walking this road of faith alone, we'll begin to realize we're not as puny as we thought we were."

David Mains, *When the Troops Are Tired*, page 129

◇ *Pray* the Tension's Good Side Prayer on page 9.

◇ *Write* down a way you've observed God ministering to or through you.

◇ *Read* chapter 7 in *When the Troops Are Tired*.

◇ *Invite* one or more people for a time of Christian hospitality.

1. According to verse 10, what is the proper relationship between fellow believers? What evidently was the situation in Corinth when Paul wrote this letter?

2. How would you summarize Paul's teaching in these verses?

3. What are some kinds of leaders people might substitute today for Paul, Cephas (Peter), and Apollos?

4. It's been said that church divisions come about more because of personality conflicts than because of doctrinal differences. Do you agree? Why or why not?

5. What are possible dangers of agreeing too readily with other believers? What about dangers of disagreeing too readily?

◇ *Pray* the Tension's Good Side Prayer on page 9.

◇ *Write* down a way you've observed God ministering to or through you on page 41.

◇ *Memorize* a verse (see *The Tapped-Out Christian's Energy Pack*).

1. Why does David praise unity so highly (see verse 3b)?

_____

2. Oil was poured on Aaron when he was anointed as a priest. It was a sign of God's blessing, and its running down on his beard and robes showed his total consecration to God's service. In what ways is this picture of blessing and consecration like unity among believers?

_____

_____

3. The heavy dew of Mount Hermon would make Mount Zion fertile and fruitful. Why might David be comparing unity with this dew?

_____

4. David compares unity to oil poured on Aaron and dew on Mount Zion. This Adventure calls unity an untapped miracle for tapped-out Christians. How is "untapped miracle" a good picture for unity?

_____

_____

5. In what ways might the beauty and blessing of unity be overlooked at times in your life at present?

_____

_____

◇ *Pray* the Tension's Good Side Prayer on page 9.

◇ *Write* down a way you've observed God ministering to or through you on page 41.

◇ *Share* with someone about how God has ministered to or through you.

◇ *Pray* for and write your pastor a note (see pp. 14–15).

1. Where was Jesus when he made this prayer, and what was about to happen to him? (See John 13:1–2.)

_____

2. Who was Jesus praying for in verses 20–24? What did he ask the Father to do for them?

_____

3. Does Jesus' prayer cause you to think differently about unity among fellow believers? If so, in what ways?

_____

_____

4. In what specific ways does lack of unity cause Christians to be tapped out?

_____

_____

5. What ministry that encourages unity among Christians could you support?

_____

> "True unity is not sought by pretending that there are no differences, ... but
> by recognizing and respecting those differences, while focusing on
> the great orthodox truths all Christians share."
>
> Charles Colson, *The Body,* page 104

◇ *Pray* the Tension's Good Side Prayer on page 9.

◇ *Write* down a way you've observed God ministering to or through you on page 41.

◇ *Read* chapter 7 in *When the Troops Are Tired.*

◇ *Practice* a fast (see pp. 16–17).

PRAY

Lord, when I feel tired and tapped out, I need to know how to tap into your resurrection power. Help me, please. Amen.

READ

Read Romans 8:28–39.

REFLECT

There's nothing quite like watching a close friend come to the Lord. Not only does it affect the life of the new believer, it impacts our life as well. Having a few conversions occur within a congregation can infuse a tired church with new spiritual vitality.

The delight of knowing the crucified and risen Christ should never grow old. When this miracle becomes ho-hum, that's deadly to the walk of faith. Christ's death and resurrection must remain the most dynamic reality in the lives of all Christians.

Many of the hardships Paul mentions in this passage were trials he'd experienced firsthand. How did he endure them? Why didn't he ever give up or become completely tapped out? The answer is that he knew the love of Christ and the power of his death and resurrection. That was an ongoing awareness for Paul.

We need to continually remind ourselves that the most important truth we know is that our Lord has died and our Lord is risen! Because the wonder of this miracle can never be exhausted, we do well to rehearse it again and again.

APPLY

1. What are the trials Paul lists that might cause a person to be tapped out?

_____

_____

2. What difficulties from your life would you add to Paul's list?

_____

_____

3. In spite of such problems, why can we consider ourselves more than conquerors? Take a few moments to meditate on verses 37–39.

_____

PRAY

Pray the Tension's Good Side Prayer.

1. What are some of the biggest accomplishments in your life? How have they helped to define who you are?

_____

_____

2. How does Paul view his accomplishments in comparison to knowing Christ? How do you view your accomplishments?

_____

_____

3. Untapped Miracle #8 in this Adventure is the Living Christ. If you were to personalize verses 10–11, how would you express your desire to know Christ better?

_____

4. Who is someone who doesn't know Christ for whom you could pray?

_____

5. What is one lesson you've learned in your relationship with Christ in the last 49 days? How can you keep growing after the Adventure ends?

_____

_____

_____

"What people want when they attend church on weekends is the assurance that Christ is truly alive.... They need to know that no matter what human leadership is in place, the risen Christ will continue with his mission."

David Mains, *When the Troops Are Tired*, page 148

◇ ***Pray*** the Tension's Good Side Prayer on page 9.

◇ ***Write*** down a way you've observed God ministering to or through you.

◇ ***Read*** chapter 8 in *When the Troops Are Tired*.

1. What evidence does Paul cite in this passage to show that we serve a risen, living Savior?

_____

_____

2. As we enter the 21st century, how does the fact that Christ is risen assure us that Christianity is still relevant?

_____

3. What are some basic spiritual needs people have today? In what ways are they similar to or different from the needs of people in Paul's day?

_____

_____

4. What are some ways Christ has met your needs in the past? How do those memories give you hope for future problems you may encounter?

_____

5. Of all the lessons you've learned during this Adventure, what miracle stands out most? Why?

_____

_____

◇ *Pray* the Tension's Good Side Prayer on page 9.

◇ *Write* down a way you've observed God ministering to or through you on page 41. How many entries does your chart have?

◇ *Complete* pages 74–75 to bring closure to your Adventure.

◇ *Share* your Adventure experience with Mainstay Church Resources (and receive a free gift). See page 79.

LOOKING BACK

Check the box if you have completed the assignment.

◇ I have completed most of Days 1–50.
◇ I have prayed the Tension's Good Side Prayer.
◇ I have recorded ways I've observed God ministering to or through me.
◇ I have talked with others about how God has ministered to or through me.
◇ I have invited one or more people for a time of Christian hospitality.
◇ I have prayed for and written my pastor a note.
◇ I have practiced a fast.
◇ I have read *When the Troops Are Tired*.
◇ I have memorized Bible verses.

Optional Follow-Up Scriptures for Extra Study on Themes 7 and 8:

◆ Galatians 5:13–26
◆ Ephesians 4:1–6
◆ John 20
◆ Revelation 1:9–18

MOVING FORWARD

Suggestions:

◆ Complete Day 51 on page 75.
◆ Continue to read Scripture and pray daily.
◆ Keep tracking how God ministers to and through you.
◆ Regularly remember your pastor in prayer.
◆ Seek opportunities to show Christian hospitality.
◆ Consider how fasting might be an ongoing part of your prayer life.
◆ Look at pages 76–77 for some helpful Adventure follow-up resources.

Your Adventure Doesn't Have to End!

Has this 50-Day Spiritual Adventure moved you closer to Christ, helped you develop healthy spiritual habits, or refreshed your devotional life? These additional resources will enable you to keep growing spiritually in the weeks and months to come.

◆ The Church You've Always Longed For
◆ What to Do When You Don't Know What to Do
◆ Facing Down Our Fears
◆ Daring to Dream Again
◆ Scripture Union Devotional Guides

For more information on these resources, see pages 76–77.

For more information on these resources, see pages 76–77.

PRAY

Lord, open my eyes to see you and my mouth to tell about you.

READ

The chief priests in Jerusalem tried to repair the damage caused by reports of Jesus' resurrection. Meanwhile, the disciples met up with the living Christ and received their first briefing on telling the world about him.

NOW READ: MATTHEW 28:11–20.

REFLECT

Lies and more lies (11–15). But you can't kill the truth with falsehood. Bribery only fosters corruption (12). A few drinks when the guards were off duty and the facts would soon be spilled. And nothing could curb the witness of those who saw, met, touched, and listened to the risen Christ and were willing to die for the privilege of serving him.

Serve him they did, as they responded to Christ's commission (18–20). To make disciples of all nations they had to go (19), and Jesus set out the program in Acts 1:8. It would be costly. But the good news was preached, disciples were made and baptized, believers were taught, and churches were established.

The challenge to make disciples of all nations is there for each of us, and whatever the cost, Jesus' promise remains true: "Surely I am with you always, to the very end of the age" (Matthew 28:20, NIV).

APPLY

During the Adventure, what is one way you were reminded that Christ is with you always (24/7)? How did he minister through you to help someone grow in him? Did sharing your *to* and *through* experiences encourage others in their faith? How could you continue to watch for and tell about Christ's 24/7 presence?

PRAY

Lord, thank you that even in my current circumstances, you can use me to help fulfill your Great Commission.

The above has been adapted for use with the 50-Day Spiritual Adventure. See the next page for more information on Discovery *or other Scripture Union devotionals.*

You've Finished the Adventure

It's Time to Make a Lifestyle Ou

Scripture Union Devotional Guides

Healthy spiritual habits like daily Scripture reading and prayer have been a part of your life for the past 50 days. Don't let them stop now!

Consider using a Scripture Union devotional guide to maintain the disciplines you've practiced throughout the Adventure. You can benefit from these devotionals all year long. And you've already been introduced to the format with the special weekend pages that introduced the Adventure themes in this journal.

There are Scripture Union devotionals for adults, teens, and children. *Quest* is available for children ages 7–10. *One to One* is for youth ages 11–14. *Discovery* is a personal application guide for mature young people and adults, and *Encounter with God* is an advanced Bible study guide. So everyone can take up the challenge of making healthy spiritual habits last all year long!

50-Day Spiritual Adventures

Try these 50-Day Adventure studies and continue the disciplines of daily Scripture reading, prayer, and challenging action steps.

◆ **The Church You've Always Longed For:**
   What You Can Do to Make It Happen
Church can be the high point of your week! In this 50-Day Spiritual Adventure, you'll discover you can contribute to building the church you've always longed for.

The Church You've Always Longed For Adult Journal and
I Like Church, But . . . necessary book—$12 for both

To order, use the form on page 78, or call weekda

Please have your VISA, MasterCard, or Discover card ready for phone orde

. Now What Do You Do?
f Growing Spiritually!

◆ **What to Do When You Don't Know What to Do:**
Trusting Christ When Life Gets Confusing
Increasingly our society is characterized by confusion. But life can be lived with perspective and direction. This Adventure will help you find practical ways to trust Christ when life gets confusing.

What to Do When You Don't Know What to Do Adult Journal and *When Life Becomes a Maze* necessary book—$12 for both

◆ **Facing Down Our Fears:**
Finding Courage When Anxiety Grips the Heart
Are there areas in your life where you feel afraid? We're all afraid of something, but don't give up just yet! In this 50-Day Spiritual Adventure, you'll find practical and biblical suggestions for finding courage and overcoming fear.

Facing Down Our Fears Adult Journal and *How to Fear God Without Being Afraid of Him* necessary book—$12 for both

◆ **Daring to Dream Again:**
Breaking Through Barriers That Hold Us Back
God has big dreams for us, but sometimes we lose sight of his great plans. Through this 50-Day Spiritual Adventure, you'll find solutions to problems that can keep you from living God's dreams.

Daring to Dream Again Adult Journal and *How to Be a World Class Christian* necessary book—$12 for both

800-224-2735 (U.S.) 1-800-461-4114 (Canada).

Mainstay Church Resources Order Form

Item	Title	Retail	Qty	Total
2810	Adult Journal	6.00	_____	_____
2860	Spanish Adult Journal	6.00	_____	_____
2820	Student Journal	6.00	_____	_____
2830	Children's Journal (3–6)	6.00	_____	_____
2840	Critter County Activity Book (K–2)	6.00	_____	_____
451K	Children's Stories & Bible Songs Tape	6.00	_____	_____
1866	When the Troops Are Tired Guidebook	6.00	1	_____
451M	When the Troops Are Tired Audiobook	13.00	_____	_____
7818	Tapped-Out Christian's Energy Pack	2.00	4	_____
1877	Life Application Study Bible, New Living Translation	40.00	_____	_____
1867	Honestly	16.00	_____	_____
1868	Roaring Lambs	11.00	_____	_____
8431	Veggie Tales—Rack, Shack, & Benny	15.00	_____	_____
1865	Open Heart, Open Home	11.00	_____	_____
1875	Partners in Prayer	11.00	_____	_____
1870	The Coming Revival	10.00	_____	_____
1871	The Power of Story	12.00	_____	_____
1872	The Body	13.00	_____	_____
5770	The Church You've Always . . . Adult Journal and book	12.00	_____	_____
5720	What to Do Adult Journal and book	12.00	_____	_____
5689	Facing Down Our Fears Adult Journal and book	12.00	_____	_____
5690	Daring to Dream Again Adult Journal and book	12.00	_____	_____
5659	Discovery (annual subscription)	20.00	_____	_____
5662	Encounter with God (annual subscription)	20.00	_____	_____
5660	One to One (annual subscription)	20.00	_____	_____
5661	Quest (annual subscription)	20.00	_____	_____

SUBTOTAL _____

Add 10% for UPS shipping/handling ($4.00 minimum) _____
Canadian or Illinois residents add 7% GST/sales tax _____
Total (subtotal + shipping + tax) _____

TOTAL AMOUNT ENCLOSED _____

Ship my order to:

Name_____

Street Address*_____ City_____

State/Prov _____ Zip/Code_____ Phone (_____) _____

*Note: UPS will not deliver to a PO box.

Mail this order form with your check made payable to:
Mainstay Church Resources, Box 30, Wheaton, IL 60189-0030
In Canada: Box 2000, Waterdown, ON L0R 2H0

For U.S. VISA, MasterCard, and Discover card orders call 1-800-224-2735. In Canada call 1-800-461-4114.

MO7ABC98

We Want to Hear from You!

Your feedback helps us evaluate the effectiveness of the Spiritual Adventure.
Please fill out this comment form and tell us what God did in your life, your
church, or your small group during this 50-day journey. In return for your feedback, we'd like to say thanks by sending you a set of free resources (shown on the
next page).

Tell us a story of how this Adventure has changed your life or the life of your
church or small group.

_____

_____

_____

_____

_____

_____

_____

_____

How can we improve the 50-Day Adventure for you?

_____

_____

_____

_____

How were you involved in the 50-Day Adventure? (Check all that apply.)

◇ Individual   ◇ Entire church

◇ Family   ◇ Small group

◇ Weekend class   ◇ Other _____

For your FREE thank-you gift, turn to the next page.

Receive Your Free Gift!

To say thanks for your feedback, we'll send you a set of three attractive full-color bookmarks with quotations on revival, a 50-Day Spiritual Adventure magnet, and your choice of one of the following Little Scripture Packs, each of which includes 23 verses.

Choose one Little Scripture Pack:

◇ The Make It Happen Little Scripture Pack for The Church You've Always Longed For

◇ The Believe It Or Not Little Scripture Pack for Trusting Christ When Life Gets Confusing

◇ The Overcome Your Fears Little Scripture Pack for Finding Courage When Anxiety Grips Your Heart

◇ The Husband's Little Scripture Pack for Marriage and Family Enrichment

◇ The Wife's Little Scripture Pack for Marriage and Family Enrichment

◇ The Parent's Little Scripture Pack for Parenting and Family Enrichment

Name_____

Street Address* _____ City_____

State/Prov _____ Zip/Code_____ Phone (_____) _____

Church Name and City_____

Radio Station on Which You Hear "Adventure Highlight" _____

Mail this comment form to:
> Mainstay Church Resources, Box 30, Wheaton, IL 60189-0030
> In Canada: Box 2000, Waterdown, ON L0R 2H0

Or, e-mail us your comments at T50DSA@AOL.com

MO7FBC98